SONG AT THE YEAR'S TURNING

SONG AT THE YEAR'S TURNING

POEMS 1942–1954

R. S. THOMAS

WITH AN INTRODUCTION BY
JOHN BETJEMAN

RUPERT HART-DAVIS
SOHO SQUARE LONDON
1955

Printed in Great Britain by Butler & Tanner Ltd., Frome and London

FOR
JAMES HANLEY

CONTENTS

THE MINISTER

page 75

LATER POEMS

ACKNOWLEDGMENTS

The author wishes to thank the editors of *Counterpoint*, *Dark Leaves*, the *Dublin Magazine*, *Encounter*, *Gangrel*, *Horizon*, *Life and Letters*, the *Listener*, the *Little Reviews Anthology*, *Modern Welsh*, *New Poems 1953*, the *New Statesman and Nation*, *Outposts*, *Poetry* (*Faber*), *Poetry* (*London*), *Time and Tide*, *The Times Literary Supplement*, *Wales*, the *Welsh Nation*, and also the B.B.C. for permission to reprint certain of the poems in this book.

INTRODUCTION

The poems of R. S. Thomas have been increasingly appreci-
ated. They are easy to understand and they improve on re-read-
ing, a sure sign of lasting quality. One of the first people to
recognize the poet's merit was Mr. Keidrych Rhys and Thomas's
first volume, *The Stones of the Field* (1946), was published by the
Druid Press, Carmarthen. That book contained the perfect
lyric, "Night and Morning". Sixteen of the thirty-seven poems
in *The Stones of the Field* have been omitted by the poet from the
present volume. From his next book, *An Acre of Land* (1952),
published by the Montgomery Printing Company, Newtown,
the poet has omitted seven poems, while *The Minister* (1953) is
reprinted in full, together with nineteen new poems.

Song at the Year's Turning therefore represents what R. S.
Thomas considers the best of his work and makes those who are
lucky enough to have the original locally-printed volumes
anxious to hold on to them. It is worth mentioning here that all
three slim books were attractively printed and produced.

In 1952 Mr. Alan Pryce-Jones commended the poetry of R. S.
Thomas on The Critics programme of the B.B.C. and the effect
was to sell out the remaining copies of the poet's work. It is rare
enough for wireless commendation appreciably to affect the sale
of any book: that it should sell out a book of poems must be
unique.

Though he is essentially a local poet, the appeal of R. S.
Thomas goes beyond the Welsh border. There certainly have
been local descriptive poets whose work will be fully enjoyed
only by those who know the locality they describe, for instance
the parson poets of the eighteenth century who wrote heroic
couplets or Thomsonian blank verse in praise of hills and ruins

in their own and neighbouring parishes. R. S. Thomas is himself a parson, the rector of a parish in Wales. He is of Welsh origin and was born in Cardiff. He taught himself Welsh when adult and his knowledge of the language helped him to understand the remote hill people who appear so clearly in these poems.

Though R. S. Thomas is a local nature poet he is not one of the escapist kind. The "wain and stook" pastoral poetry of the neo-Georgians, good as much of it was, was literary and one associates it with thick paper and woodcuts of the home counties. R. S. Thomas is not at all literary and even remoter from the neo-Georgians than he is from the pastoral poets of the eighteenth century.

Having said so much about what sort of a nature poet he is not, makes it easier to describe the man revealed in the poems. R. S. Thomas is a country priest. He went to his parish not to bury himself in literature and take only the statutory services, but to learn all about his inarticulate and no doubt sometimes suspicious parishioners. He went with a keen interest in natural history and birds, in scenery, agriculture and the agricultural way of life. By talking to his parishioners in their own language about the things they knew, he would win the souls to the Christian faith and the sacraments. This much is implicit in many of his poems, though in none of them is it explicitly stated. This is what makes him look at man and nature in the light of eternity. Consider his description of "The Village":

> So little happens; the black dog
> Cracking his fleas in the hot sun
> Is history. Yet the girl who crosses
> From door to door moves to a scale
> Beyond the bland day's two dimensions.
>
> Stay, then, village, for round you spins
> On slow axis a world as vast
> And meaningful as any poised
> By great Plato's solitary mind.

Compare that with Samuel Lewis's description of Manafon where R. S. Thomas was rector from 1942 until last year when he accepted a living in another country part of Wales. Lewis published his topographical dictionary of Wales in 1840, but the village of Manafon is likely to have changed little since Lewis's day. Then as now it is "in a mountainous district nearly in the centre of the county, and intersected by the river Rhiw, and also by the road leading from Llanvair to Newtown and Montgomery: it comprises an extensive tract of land of which a considerable portion is uncultivated, and of the remainder, one half consists of old enclosures, and the other has been enclosed and brought into a state of cultivation under the provision of an act of parliament obtained in 1796. The surrounding scenery is strikingly diversified, and from the higher grounds are obtained extensive and pleasingly varied prospects." R. S. Thomas breathes the wind and the wild flowers into this estate agent's language. What sweat went to bringing those enclosures into cultivation may be gathered from "The Airy Tomb". What pathos there is in the hard hill life may be seen in a poem like "Farm Child".

A feeling for Dissent in R. S. Thomas's poetry gives it a peculiar Welshness. Because he identifies the wild beauty of his parish with the lives and work of its parishioners whom he loves, he cannot disregard that nonconformity which is still stronger in Wales than the Church. Under "Manafon", Samuel Lewis mentions that a Sunday school run by the Church has from thirty to sixty children according to the season of the year, of whom four are educated free and the rest pay. On the other hand, "the Calvinistic Methodists gratuitously teach from a hundred to two hundred males and females in three Sunday schools". R. S. Thomas describes the fruit of that teaching in his long poem "The Minister" which was written for broadcasting. Here, one feels, but for the fact that he loved the beauty of Welsh scenery and pitied rather than despised those who cannot look up from the barren soil and their hard tasks, goes R. S. Thomas.

There have been good Welsh writers driven to satire and contempt by the narrow Calvinism of a mercenary peasantry. Poor Morgan, the minister of this poem, was well versed in Calvin's theology and mistrusted beauty in scenery or women. So he fell to railing against sin and leaving out charity until his heart was twisted and he died defeated by his own fierce creed.

> Is there no passion in Wales? There is none
> Except in the racked hearts of men like Morgan
> Condemned to wither and starve in the cramped cell
> Of thought their fathers made them.
> Protestantism—the adroit castrator
> Of art; the bitter negation
> Of song and dance and the heart's innocent joy—
> You have botched our flesh and left us only the soul's
> Terrible impotence in a warm world.

W. B. Yeats seems to have been the only recent writer to have made an acknowledged impression on R. S. Thomas's style. He thinks that poetry should be read to oneself not out loud and that it is heard by an inner ear. He does not read nineteenth-century poems because he thinks that their obvious and jingly rhythms might upset his own sense of metre.

This retiring poet had no wish for an introduction to be written to his poems, but his publisher believed that a "name" was needed to help sell the book. The "name" which has the honour to introduce this fine poet to a wider public will be forgotten long before that of R. S. Thomas.

JOHN BETJEMAN

The Stones of the Field

For thou shalt be in league with the stones of the field

BOOK OF JOB

The Stones of the Field was first published in 1946 by the Druid Press, Carmarthen.

OUT OF THE HILLS

Dreams clustering thick on his sallow skull,
Dark as curls, he comes, ambling with his cattle
From the starved pastures. He has shaken from off his
    shoulders
The weight of the sky, and the lash of the wind's sharpness
Is healing already under the medicinal sun.
Clouds of cattle breath, making the air heady,
Remember the summer's sweetness, the wet road runs
Blue as a river before him; the legendary town
Dreams of his coming; under the half-closed lids
Of the indolent shops sleep dawdles, emptying the last
Tankards of darkness, before the officious light
Bundles it up the chimney out of sight.

The shadow of the mountain dwindles; his scaly eye
Sloughs its cold care and glitters. The day is his
To dabble a finger in, and, merry as crickets,
A chorus of coins sings in his tattered pockets.
Shall we follow him down, witness his swift undoing
In the indifferent streets: the sudden disintegration
Of his soul's hardness, traditional discipline
Of flint and frost thawing in ludicrous showers
Of maudlin laughter; the limpid runnels of speech
Sullied and slurred, as the beer-glass chimes the hours?
No, wait for him here. At midnight he will return,
Threading the tunnel that contains the dawn
Of all his fears. Be then his fingerpost
Homeward. The earth is patient; he is not lost.

A LABOURER

Who can tell his years, for the winds have stretched
So tight the skin on the bare racks of bone
That his face is smooth, inscrutable as stone?
And when he wades in the brown bilge of earth
Hour by hour, or stoops to pull
The reluctant swedes, who can read the look
In the colourless eye, as his back comes straight
Like an old tree lightened of the snow's weight?
Is there love there, or hope, or any thought
For the frail form broken beneath his tread,
And the sweet pregnancy that yields his bread?

HOMO SAPIENS 1941

Murmuration of engines in the cold caves of air,
And, daring the starlight above the stiff sea of cloud,
Deadly as a falcon brooding over its prey
In a tower of spirit-dazzling and splendid light,
Pedestrian man holds grimly on his way.
Legions of winds, ambushed in crystal corries,
Conspiring to destroy him, and hosts of ice,
Thronging him close, weigh down his delicate wings;
But loud as a drum in his ear the hot blood sings,
And a frenzy of solitude mantles him like a god.

A THOUGHT FROM NIETZSCHE

Ah, body, white body, my poor pelt;
Lean acre of ground that the years master,
Though fenced cunningly from wind and cold;
What bird sings deep in your leafless boughs,
What flowers adorn your terraces of bone?
You are scrub, you are desert, you are dry sand,
In whose bare banks the blood stream bickers in vain.
You are betrayed by wilderness within,
That spreads upward and outward like a stain.

A PEASANT

Iago Prytherch his name, though, be it allowed,
Just an ordinary man of the bald Welsh hills,
Who pens a few sheep in a gap of cloud.
Docking mangels, chipping the green skin
From the yellow bones with a half-witted grin
Of satisfaction, or churning the crude earth
To a stiff sea of clods that glint in the wind—
So are his days spent, his spittled mirth
Rarer than the sun that cracks the cheeks
Of the gaunt sky perhaps once in a week.
And then at night see him fixed in his chair
Motionless, except when he leans to gob in the fire.
There is something frightening in the vacancy of his
    mind.
His clothes, sour with years of sweat
And animal contact, shock the refined,
But affected, sense with their stark naturalness.
Yet this is your prototype, who, season by season
Against siege of rain and the wind's attrition,
Preserves his stock, an impregnable fortress
Not to be stormed even in death's confusion.
Remember him, then, for he, too, is a winner of wars,
Enduring like a tree under the curious stars.

COUNTRY CHILD

Dropped without joy from the gaunt womb he lies,
Maturing in his place against his parents' ageing;
The slow scene unfolds before his luckless eyes
To the puckered window, where the cold storm's raging
Curtains the world, and the grey curlew cries,
Uttering a grief too sharp for the breast's assuaging.

So the days will drift into months and the months to years,
Moulding his mouth to silence, his hand to the plough;
And the world will grow to a few lean acres of grass,
And an orchard of stars in the night's unscaleable boughs.
But see at the bare field's edge, where he'll surely pass,
An ash tree wantons with sensuous body and smooth,
Provocative limbs to play the whore to his youth,
Till hurled with hot haste into manhood he woos and weds
A wife half wild, half shy of the ancestral bed,
The crumbling house, and the whisperers on the stairs.

THE RISING OF GLYNDŴR

Thunder-browed and shaggy-throated
All the men were there,
And the women with the hair
That is the raven's and the rook's despair.

Winds awoke, and vixen-footed
Firelight prowled the glade;
The stars were hooded and the moon afraid
To vex the darkness with her yellow braid.

Then he spoke, and anger kindled
In each brooding eye;
Swords and spears accused the sky,
The woods resounded with a bitter cry.

Beasts gave tongue and brown owls hooted,
Every branch grew loud
With the menace of that crowd,
That thronged the dark, huge as a thundercloud.

NIGHT AND MORNING

One night of tempest I arose and went
Along the Menai shore on dreaming bent;
The wind was strong, and savage swung the tide,
And the waves blustered on Caernarfon side.

But on the morrow, when I passed that way,
On Menai shore the hush of heaven lay;
The wind was gentle and the sea a flower,
And the sun slumbered on Caernarfon tower.

(From the Welsh Traditional)

AFFINITY

Consider this man in the field beneath,
Gaitered with mud, lost in his own breath,
Without joy, without sorrow,
Without children, without wife,
Stumbling insensitively from furrow to furrow,
A vague somnambulist; but hold your tears,
For his name also is written in the Book of Life.

Ransack your brainbox, pull out the drawers
That rot in your heart's dust, and what have you to
    give
To enrich his spirit or the way he lives?
From the standpoint of education or caste or creed
Is there anything to show that your essential need
Is less than his, who has the world for church,
And stands bare-headed in the woods' wide porch
Morning and evening to hear God's choir
Scatter their praises? Don't be taken in
By stinking garments or an aimless grin;
He also is human, and the same small star,
That lights you homeward, has inflamed his mind
With the old hunger, born of his kind.

SONG

We, who are men, how shall we know
Earth's ecstasy, who feels the plough
Probing her womb,
And after, the sweet gestation
And the year's care for her condition?
We, who have forgotten, so long ago
It happened, our own orgasm,
When the wind mixed with our limbs
And the sun had suck at our bosom;
We, who have affected the livery
Of the times' prudery,
How shall we quicken again
To the lust and thrust of the sun
And the seedling rain?

COUNTRY CHURCH

(*Manafon*)

The church stands, built from the river stone,
Brittle with light, as though a breath could shatter
Its slender frame, or spill the limpid water,
Quiet as sunlight, cupped within the bone.

It stands yet. But though soft flowers break
In delicate waves round limbs the river fashioned
With so smooth care, no friendly God has cautioned
The brimming tides of fescue for its sake.

PEASANT GREETING

No speech; the raised hand affirms
All that is left unsaid
By the mute tongue and the unmoistened lips:
The land's patience and a tree's
Knotted endurance and
The heart's doubt whether to curse or bless,
All packed into a single gesture.
The knees crumble to the downward pull
Of the harsh earth, the eyes,
Fuddled with coldness, have no skill to smile.
Life's bitter jest is hollow, mirthless he slips
To his long grave under the wave of wind,
That breaks continually on the brittle ear.

A PRIEST TO HIS PEOPLE

Men of the hills, wantoners, men of Wales,
With your sheep and your pigs and your ponies, your sweaty
    females,
How I have hated you for your irreverence, your scorn even
Of the refinements of art and the mysteries of the Church,
I whose invective would spurt like a flame of fire
To be quenched always in the coldness of your stare.
Men of bone, wrenched from the bitter moorland,
Who have not yet shaken the moss from your savage skulls,
Or prayed the peat from your eyes,
Did you detect like an ewe or an ailing wether,
Driven into the undergrowth by the nagging flies,
My true heart wandering in a wood of lies?

You are curt and graceless, yet your sudden laughter
Is sharp and bright as a whipped pool,
When the wind strikes or the clouds are flying;
And all the devices of church and school
Have failed to cripple your unhallowed movements,
Or put a halter on your wild soul.
You are lean and spare, yet your strength is a mockery
Of the pale words in the black Book,
And why should you come like sparrows for prayer crumbs,
Whose hands can dabble in the world's blood?

I have taxed your ignorance of rhyme and sonnet,
Your want of deference to the painter's skill,
But I know, as I listen, that your speech has in it
The source of all poetry, clear as a rill
Bubbling from your lips; and what brushwork could equal
The artistry of your dwelling on the bare hill?
You will forgive, then, my initial hatred,
My first intolerance of your uncouth ways,

You who are indifferent to all that I can offer,
Caring not whether I blame or praise.
With your pigs and your sheep and your sons
        and holly-cheeked daughters
You will still continue to unwind your days
In a crude tapestry under the jealous heavens
To affront, bewilder, yet compel my gaze.

MADRIGAL

Your love is dead, lady, your love is dead;
Dribbles no sound
From his stopped lips, though swift underground
Spurts his wild hair.

Your love is dead, lady, your love is dead;
Faithless he lies
Deaf to your call, though shades of his eyes
Break through and stare.

ON A PORTRAIT OF JOSEPH HONE
BY AUGUSTUS JOHN

As though the brute eyes had seen
In the hushed meadows the weasel,
That would tear the soft down of the throat
And suck the veins dry
Of their glittering blood.

And the mouth formed to the cry,
That gushed from the cleft heart
And flowed coldly as spring water over
The stone lips.

AN OLD MAN

Looking upon this tree with its quaint pretension
Of holding the earth, a leveret, in its claws,
Or marking the texture of its living bark,
A grey sea wrinkled by the winds of years,
I understand whence this man's body comes,
Its veins and fibres, the bare boughs of bone,
The trellised thicket, where the heart, that robin,
Greets with a song the seasons of the blood.

But where in meadow or mountain shall I match
The individual accent of the speech
That is the ear's familiar? To what sun attribute
The honeyed warmness of his smile?
To which of the deciduous brood is german
The angel peeping from the latticed eye?

THE CRY OF ELISHA AFTER ELIJAH

The chariot of Israel came,
And the bold, beautiful knights,
To free from his close prison
The friend who was my delight;
Cold is my cry over the vast deep shaken,
Bereft was I, for he was taken.

Through the straight places of Baca
We went with an equal will,
Not knowing who would emerge
First from that gloomy vale;
Cold is my cry; our bond was broken,
Bereft was I, for he was taken.

Where, then, came they to rest,
Those steeds and that car of fire?
My understanding is darkened,
It is no gain to enquire;
Better to await the long night's ending,
Till the light comes, far truths transcending.

I yield, since no wisdom lies
In seeking to go his way;
A man without knowledge am I
Of the quality of his joy;
Yet living souls, a prodigious number,
Bright-faced as dawn, invest God's chamber.

The friends that we loved well,
Though they vanished far from our sight,

In a new country were found
Beyond this vale of night;
O blest are they, without pain or fretting
In the sun's light that knows no setting.
(*From the Welsh of Thomas Williams, Bethesda'r Fro*)

IRE

Are you out, woman of the lean pelt,
And the table unlaid and bare
As a boar's backside, and the kettle
Loud as an old man, plagued with spittle,
Or a cat fight upon the stair?
The sink stinks, and the floor unscrubbed
Is no mirror for the preening sun
At the cracked lattice. Oh, the oven's cold
As Jesus' church, and never a bun
Lurks in the larder—Is this the way
You welcome your man from his long mowing
Of the harsh, unmannerly, mountain hay?

THE AIRY TOMB

Twm was a dunce at school, and was whipped and shaken
More than I care to say, but without avail,
For where one man can lead a horse to the pail
Twenty can't make him drink what is not to his mind,
And books and sums were poison to Tomos, he was stone
    blind
To the printer's magic; yet his grass-green eye
Missed neither swoop nor swerve of the hawk's wing
Past the high window, and the breeze could bring,
Above the babble of the room's uproar,
Songs to his ear from the sun-dusted moor,
The grey curlew's whistle and the shrill, far cry
Of circling buzzard . . . This was Twm at school,
Subject to nothing but the sky and the wind's rule.
And then at fourteen term ended and the lad was free.
Scatheless as when he entered, he could write and spell
No more than the clouds could or the dribbling rain,
That scrawled vague messages on the window pane.

And so he returned to the Bwlch to help his father
With the rough work of the farm, to ditch, and gather
The slick ewes from the hill; to milk the cow,
And coax the mare that dragged the discordant plough.
Stepping with one stride thus from boy to man,
His school books finished with, he now began
Learning what none could teach but the hill people
In that cold country, where grass and tree
Are a green heritage more rich and rare
Than a queen's emerald or an untouched maid.
It were as well to bring the tup to the wild mare,
Or put the heron and the hen to couple,
As mate a stranger from the fat plain
With that gaunt wilderness, where snow is laid

37

Deadly as leprosy till the first of May,
And a man counts himself lucky if All Saints' Day
Finds his oats hived in the tottering barn.
But Tomos took to the life like a hillman born;
His work was play after the dull school, and hands,
Shamed by the pen's awkwardness, toyed with the fleece
Of ewe and wether; eyes found a new peace
Tracing the poems, which the rooks wrote in the sky.

So his shadow lengthened, and the years sped by
With the wind's quickness; Twm had turned nineteen,
When his father sickened and at the week's end died,
Leaving him heir to the lean patch of land,
Pinned to the hill-top, and the cloudy acres,
Kept as a sheep-walk. At his mother's side
He stood in the graveyard, where the undertaker
Sprinkled earth rubble with a loud tattoo
On the cheap coffin; but his heart was hurt
By the gash in the ground, and too few, too few,
Were the tears that he dropped for that lonely man
Beginning his journey to annihilation.
He had seen sheep rotting in the wind and sun,
And a hawk floating in a bubbling pool,
Its weedy entrails mocking the breast
Laced with bright water; but the dead and living
Moved hand in hand on the mountain crest
In the calm circle of taking and giving.
A wide sepulchre of brisk, blue air
Was the beast's portion, but a mortal's lot
The board's strictness, and an ugly scar
On the earth's surface, till the deliberate sod
Sealed off for ever the green land he trod.

But the swift grass, that covered the unsightly wound
In the prim churchyard, healed Tomos' mind

Of its grave-sickness, and December shadows
Dwindled to nothingness in the spring meadows,
That were blowsy with orchis and the loose bog-cotton.
Then the sun strengthened and the hush of June
Settled like lichen on the thick-timbered house,
Where Twm and his mother ate face to face
At the bare table, and each tick of the clock
Was a nail knocked in the lid of the coffin
Of that pale, spent woman, who sat with death
Jogging her elbow through the hot, still days
Of July and August, or passed like a ghost
By the scurrying poultry—it was ever her boast
Not to stay one winter with the goodman cold
In his callous bed. Twm was bumpkin blind
To the vain hysteria of a woman's mind,
And prated of sheep fairs, but the first frost came
To prove how ungarnished was the truth she told.

Can you picture Tomos now in the house alone,
The room silent, and the last mourner gone
Down the hill pathway? Did he sit by the flame
Of his turf fire and watch till dawn
The slow crumbling of the world he had known?
Did he rebuild out of the ragged embers
A new life, tempered to the sting of sorrow?
Twm went to bed and woke on the grey morrow
To the usual jobbery in sty and stable;
Cleaned out the cow-house, harnessed the mare,
And went prospecting with the keen ploughshare.
Yet sometimes the day was dark, and the clouds remembered,
Herded in the bare lanes of sky, the funeral rite,
And Tomos about the house or set at table
Was aware of something for which he had no name,
Though the one tree, which dripped through the winter
    night

With a clock's constancy, tried hard to tell
The insensitive mind what the heart knew well.

But March squalls, making the windows rattle,
Blew great gaps in his thoughts, till April followed
With a new sweetness, that set the streams gossiping.
On Easter Day he heard the first warbler sing
In the quick ash by the door, and the snow made room
On the sharp turf for the first fumbling lamb.
Docking and grading now until after dark
In the green field or fold, there was too much work
For the mind to wander, though the robin wove
In the young hazel a sweet tale of love.
And what is love to an uncultured youth
In the desolate pastures, but the itch of cattle
At set times and seasons? Twm rarely went down
With his gay neighbours to the petticoat town
In a crook of the valley, and his mind was free
Of the dream pictures which lead to romance.
Hearts and arrows, scribbled at the lane's entrance,
Were a meaningless symbol, as esoteric
As his school fractions; the one language he knew
Was the shrill scream in the dark, the shadow within the
    shadow,
The glimmer of flesh, deadly as mistletoe.

Of course there was talk in the parish, girls stood at their
    doors
In November evenings, their glances busy as moths
Round that far window; and some, whom passion made
    bolder
As the buds opened, lagged in the bottom meadow
And coughed and called. But never a voice replied
From that grim house, nailed to the mountain side,

For Tomos was up with the lambs, or stealthily hoarding
The last light from the sky in his soul's crannies.
So the tongues still wagged, and Tomos became a story
To please a neighbour with, or raise the laughter
In the lewd tavern, for folk cannot abide
The inscrutable riddle, posed by their own kin.
And you, hypocrite reader, at ease in your chair,
Do not mock their conduct, for are you not also weary
Of this odd tale, preferring the usual climax?
He was not well-favoured, you think, nor gay, nor rich,
But surely it happened that one of those supple bitches
With the sly haunches angled him into her net
At the male season, or, what is perhaps more romantic,
Some lily-white maid, a clerk or a minister's daughter,
With delicate hands, and eyes brittle as flowers
Or curved sea-shells, taught him the tender airs
Of a true gallant?
           No, no, you must face the fact
Of his long life alone in that crumbling house
With winds rending the joints, and the grey rain's claws
Sharp in the thatch; of his work up on the moors
With the moon for candle, and the shrill rabble of stars
Crowding his shoulders. For Twm was true to his fate,
That wound solitary as a brook through the crimson heather,
Trodden only by sheep, where youth and age
Met in the circle of a buzzard's flight
Round the blue axle of heaven; and a fortnight gone
Was the shy soul from the festering flesh and bone
When they found him there, entombed in the lucid weather.

An Acre of Land

Nid câr da ond acer o dir
SIÔN TUDUR 16TH CENT.

An Acre of Land was first published in 1952 by the Montgomery Printing Company, Newtown.

MEMORIES

Come, Iago, my friend, and let us stand together
Now in the time of the mild weather,
Before the wind changes and the winter brings
The leprous frost to the fields, and I will sing
The land's praises, making articulate
Your strong feelings, your thoughts of no date,
Your secret learning, innocent of books.
Do you remember the shoals of wheat, the look
Of the prawned barley, and the hissing swarm
Of winged oats busy about the warm
Stalks? Or the music of the taut scythe
Breaking in regular waves upon the lithe
Limbs of the grass? Do you recall the days
Of the young spring with lambs mocking the snow
That was patched with green and gold in the bare fields?
Or the autumn nights with Sirius loud as a bird
In the wood's darkness?

                  Yes, though your lips are sealed
By a natural reticence, your eyes betray
The heart's rich harvest, gathered seasons ago
When I was a child too small even to have heard
Under the sombre foliage of the sky
The owl and badger answering my cry.

THE WELSH HILL COUNTRY

Too far for you to see
The fluke and the foot-rot and the fat maggot
Gnawing the skin from the small bones,
The sheep are grazing at Bwlch-y-Fedwen,
Arranged romantically in the usual manner
On a bleak background of bald stone.

Too far for you to see
The moss and the mould on the cold chimneys,
The nettles growing through the cracked doors,
The houses stand empty at Nant-yr-Eira,
There are holes in the roofs that are thatched with
        sunlight,
And the fields are reverting to the bare moor.

Too far, too far to see
The set of his eyes and the slow phthisis
Wasting his frame under the ripped coat,
There's a man still farming at Ty'n-y-Fawnog,
Contributing grimly to the accepted pattern,
The embryo music dead in his throat.

WALES

Listen, listen! Where the river fastens
The trees together with a blue thread,
I hear the ousel of Cilgwri telling
The mournful story of the long dead.

Above the clatter of the broken water
The song is caught in the bare boughs;
The very air is veined with darkness, hearken!
The brown owl wakens in the woods now.

The owl, the ousel, and the toad's carousal
In Cors Fochno of the old laws—
I hear them yet, but in what thicket cowers
Gwernabwy's eagle with the sharp claws?

SONG FOR GWYDION

When I was a child and the soft flesh was forming
Quietly as snow on the bare boughs of bone,
My father brought me trout from the green river
From whose chill lips the water song had flown.

Dull grew their eyes, the beautiful, blithe garland
Of stipples faded, as light shocked the brain;
They were the first sweet sacrifice I tasted,
A young god, ignorant of the blood's stain.

THE EVACUEE

She woke up under a loose quilt
Of leaf patterns, woven by the light
At the small window, busy with the boughs
Of a young cherry; but wearily she lay,
Waiting for the syren, slow to trust
Nature's deceptive peace, and then afraid
Of the long silence, she would have crept
Uneasily from the bedroom with its frieze
Of fresh sunlight, had not a cock crowed,
Shattering the surface of that limpid pool
Of stillness, and before the ripples died
One by one in the field's shallows,
The farm awoke with uninhibited din.

And now the noise and not the silence drew her
Down the bare stairs at great speed.
The sounds and voices were a rough sheet
Waiting to catch her, as though she leaped
From a scorched story of the charred past.

And there the table and the gallery
Of farm faces trying to be kind
Beckoned her nearer, and she sat down
Under an awning of salt hams.

And so she grew, a small bird in the nest
Of welcome that was built about her,
Home now after so long away
In the flowerless streets of the drab town.
The men watched her busy with the hens,
The soft flesh ripening warm as corn

On the sticks of limbs, the grey eyes clear,
Rinsed with dew of their long dread.
The men watched her, and, nodding, smiled
With earth's charity, patient and strong.

THE ANCIENTS OF THE WORLD

The salmon lying in the depths of Llyn Llifon,
  Secretly as a thought in a dark mind,
Is not so old as the owl of Cwm Cowlyd
  Who tells her sorrow nightly on the wind.

The ousel singing in the woods of Cilgwri,
  Tirelessly as a stream over the mossed stones,
Is not so old as the toad of Cors Fochno
  Who feels the cold skin sagging round his bones.

The toad and the ousel and the stag of Rhedynfre,
  That has cropped each leaf from the tree of life,
Are not so old as the owl of Cwm Cowlyd,
  That the proud eagle would have to wife.

DEPOPULATION OF THE HILLS

Leave it, leave it—the hole under the door
Was a mouth through which the rough wind spoke
Ever more sharply; the dank hand
Of age was busy on the walls
Scrawling in blurred characters
Messages of hate and fear.

Leave it, leave it—the cold rain began
At summer end—there is no road
Over the bog, and winter comes
With mud above the axletree.

Leave it, leave it—the rain dripped
Day and night from the patched roof
Sagging beneath its load of sky.

Did the earth help them, time befriend
These last survivors? Did the spring grass
Heal winter's ravages? The grass
Wrecked them in its draughty tides,
Grew from the chimney-stack like smoke,
Burned its way through the weak timbers.
That was nature's jest, the sides
Of the old hulk cracked, but not with mirth.

THE GAP IN THE HEDGE

That man, Prytherch, with the torn cap,
I saw him often, framed in the gap
Between two hazels with his sharp eyes,
Bright as thorns, watching the sunrise
Filling the valley with its pale yellow
Light, where the sheep and the lambs went haloed
With grey mist lifting from the dew.
Or was it a likeness that the twigs drew
With bold pencilling upon that bare
Piece of the sky? For he's still there
At early morning, when the light is right
And I look up suddenly at a bird's flight.

CYNDDYLAN ON A TRACTOR

Ah, you should see Cynddylan on a tractor.
Gone the old look that yoked him to the soil;
He's a new man now, part of the machine,
His nerves of metal and his blood oil.
The clutch curses, but the gears obey
His least bidding, and lo, he's away
Out of the farmyard, scattering hens.
Riding to work now as a great man should,
He is the knight at arms breaking the fields'
Mirror of silence, emptying the wood
Of foxes and squirrels and bright jays.
The sun comes over the tall trees
Kindling all the hedges, but not for him
Who runs his engine on a different fuel.
And all the birds are singing, bills wide in vain,
As Cynddylan passes proudly up the lane.

THE HILL FARMER SPEAKS

I am the farmer, stripped of love
And thought and grace by the land's hardness;
But what I am saying over the fields'
Desolate acres, rough with dew,
Is, Listen, listen, I am a man like you.

The wind goes over the hill pastures
Year after year, and the ewes starve,
Milkless, for want of the new grass.
And I starve, too, for something the spring
Can never foster in veins run dry.

The pig is a friend, the cattle's breath
Mingles with mine in the still lanes;
I wear it willingly like a cloak
To shelter me from your curious gaze.

The hens go in and out at the door
From sun to shadow, as stray thoughts pass
Over the floor of my wide skull.
The dirt is under my cracked nails ;
The tale of my life is smirched with dung ;
The phlegm rattles.   But what I am saying
Over the grasses rough with dew
Is, Listen, listen, I am a man like you.

THE TREE

Owain Glyn Dŵr Speaks

Gruffudd Llwyd put into my head
The strange thought, singing of the dead
In *awdl* and *cywydd* to the harp,
As though he plucked with each string
The taut fibres of my being.
Accustomed to Iolo and his praise
Of Sycharth with its brown beer,
Meat from the chase, fish from the weir,
Its proud women sipping wine,
I had equated the glib bards
With flattery and the expected phrase,
Tedious concomitants of power.
But Gruffudd Llwyd with his theme
Of old princes in whose veins
Swelled the same blood that sweetened mine
Pierced my lethargy, I heard
Above the tuneful consonants
The sharp anguish, the despair
Of men beyond my smooth domain
Fretting under the barbed sting
Of English law, starving among
The sleek woods no longer theirs.
And I remembered that old nurse
Prating of omens in the sky
When I was born, the heavens inflamed
With meteors and the stars awry.
I shunned the thought, there was the claim
Of wife and young ones, my first care,
And Sycharth, too; I would dismiss
Gruffudd.   But something in his song
Stopped me, held me; the bright harp

Was strung with fire, the music burned
All but the one green thought away.
The thought grew to a great tree
In the full spring time of the year;
The far tribes rallied to its green
Banner waving in the wind;
Its roots were nourished with their blood.
And days were fair under those boughs;
The dawn foray, the dusk carouse
Bred the stout limb and blither heart
That marked us of Llywelyn's brood.
It was with us as with the great;
For one brief hour the summer came
To the tree's branches and we heard
In the green shade Rhiannon's birds
Singing tirelessly as the streams
That pluck glad tunes from the grey stones
Of Powys of the broken hills.

The music ceased, the obnoxious wind
And frost of autumn picked the leaves
One by one from the gaunt boughs;
They fell, some in a gold shower
About its roots, but some were hurled
Out of my sight, out of my power,
Over the face of the grim world.

It is winter still in the bare tree
That sprang from the seed which Gruffudd sowed
In my hot brain in the long nights
Of wine and music on the hearth
Of Sycharth of the open gates.
But here at its roots I watch and wait
For the new spring so long delayed;
And he who stands in the light above

And sets his ear to the scarred bole,
Shall hear me tell from the deep tomb
How sorrow may bud the tree with tears,
But only his blood can make it bloom.

DEATH OF A PEASANT

You remember Davies? He died, you know,
With his face to the wall, as the manner is
Of the poor peasant in his stone croft
On the Welsh hills. I recall the room
Under the slates, and the smirched snow
Of the wide bed in which he lay,
Lonely as an ewe that is sick to lamb
In the hard weather of mid–March.
I remember also the trapped wind
Tearing the curtains, and the wild light's
Frequent hysteria upon the floor,
The bare floor without a rug
Or mat to soften the loud tread
Of neighbours crossing the uneasy boards
To peer at Davies with gruff words
Of meaningless comfort, before they turned
Heartless away from the stale smell
Of death in league with those dank walls.

THE MIXEN

Yes, I forgot the mixen,
Its crude colour and tart smell.
I described him fondly but not well
In showing his eyes blue as flowers,
His hair like the crow's wing,
His easy movements over the acres
Ploughed ready for the stars' sowing.
I sang him early in the fields
With dew embroidered, but forgot
The mixen clinging to his heel,
Its brand under the ripped coat,
The mixen slurring his strong speech.
I made him comely but too rich;
The mixen sours the dawn's gold.

WELSH HISTORY

We were a people taut for war; the hills
Were no harder, the thin grass
Clothed them more warmly than the coarse
Shirts our small bones.
We fought, and were always in retreat,
Like snow thawing upon the slopes
Of Mynydd Mawr; and yet the stranger
Never found our ultimate stand
In the thick woods, declaiming verse
To the sharp prompting of the harp.

Our kings died, or they were slain
By the old treachery at the ford.
Our bards perished, driven from the halls
Of nobles by the thorn and bramble.

We were a people bred on legends,
Warming our hands at the red past.
The great were ashamed of our loose rags
Clinging stubbornly to the proud tree
Of blood and birth, our lean bellies
And mud houses were a proof
Of our ineptitude for life.

We were a people wasting ourselves
In fruitless battles for our masters,
In lands to which we had no claim,
With men for whom we felt no hatred.

We were a people, and are so yet.
When we have finished quarrelling for crumbs
Under the table, or gnawing the bones
Of a dead culture, we will arise,
Armed, but not in the old way.

SONG

Wandering, wandering, hoping to find
The ring of mushrooms with the wet rind,
Cold to the touch, but bright with dew,
A green asylum from time's range.

And finding instead the harsh ways
Of the ruinous wind and the clawed rain;
The storm's hysteria in the bush;
The wild creatures and their pain.

WELSH LANDSCAPE

To live in Wales is to be conscious
At dusk of the spilled blood
That went to the making of the wild sky,
Dyeing the immaculate rivers
In all their courses.
It is to be aware,
Above the noisy tractor
And hum of the machine
Of strife in the strung woods,
Vibrant with sped arrows.
You cannot live in the present,
At least not in Wales.
There is the language for instance,
The soft consonants
Strange to the ear.
There are cries in the dark at night
As owls answer the moon,
And thick ambush of shadows,
Hushed at the fields' corners
There is no present in Wales,
And no future;
There is only the past,
Brittle with relics,
Wind-bitten towers and castles
With sham ghosts;
Mouldering quarries and mines;
And an impotent people,
Sick with inbreeding,
Worrying the carcase of an old song.

SOIL

A field with tall hedges and a young
Moon in the branches and one star
Declining westward set the scene
Where he works slowly astride the rows
Of red mangolds and green swedes
Plying mechanically his cold blade.

This is his world, the hedge defines
The mind's limits; only the sky
Is boundless, and he never looks up;
His gaze is deep in the dark soil,
As are his feet. The soil is all;
His hands fondle it, and his bones
Are formed out of it with the swedes.
And if sometimes the knife errs,
Burying itself in his shocked flesh,
Then out of the wound the blood seeps home
To the warm soil from which it came.

VALEDICTION

You failed me, farmer, I was afraid you would
The day I saw you loitering with the cows,
Yourself one of them but for the smile,
Vague as moonlight, cast upon your face
From some dim source, whose nature I mistook.
The hills had grace, the light clothed them
With wild beauty, so that I thought,
Watching the pattern of your slow wake
Through seas of dew, that you yourself
Wore that same beauty by the right of birth.

I know now, many a time since
Hurt by your spite or guile that is more sharp
Than stinging hail and treacherous
As white frost forming after a day
Of smiling warmth, that your uncouthness has
No kinship with the earth, where all is forgiven,
All is requited in the seasonal round
Of sun and rain, healing the year's scars.

Unnatural and inhuman, your wild ways
Are not sanctioned; you are condemned
By man's potential stature.   The two things
That could redeem your ignorance, the beauty
And grace that trees and flowers labour to teach,
Were never yours, you shut your heart against them.
You stopped your ears to the soft influence
Of birds, preferring the dull tone
Of the thick blood, the loud, unlovely rattle
Of mucous in the throat, the shallow stream
Of neighbours' trivial talk.

For this I leave you
Alone in your harsh acres, herding pennies
Into a sock to serve you for a pillow
Through the long night that waits upon your span.

SUMMER

You would think sometimes that summer never comes
To the farmer in his fields, stripped by the wind
To the blue bone, or impotent with snow.
You have become used to his ascetic form
Moving within its cell of leafless trees.
Not so; his blood uncurls with the slow sap,
Stretching itself among its sinuous boughs;
His blood grows hot, the singing cloak of flies,
Worn each day, bears witness; the stones ring
Fierce echoes of his heat; he meets himself
Everywhere in the smell of the ripe earth.

ENIGMA

A man is in the fields, let us look with his eyes,
As the first clouds ripen with the sunrise,
At the earth around us, marking the nameless flowers
That minister to him through the tedious hours
Of sweat and toil, their grave, half-human faces
Lifted in vain to greet him where he passes.
The wind ruffles the meadow, the tall clouds sail
Westward full-rigged, and darken with their shadow
The bright surface as a thought the mind.
The earth is beautiful, and he is blind
To it all, or notices only the weeds' way
Of wrestling with and choking the young hay
That pushes tentatively from the gaunt womb.
He cannot read the flower-printed book
Of nature, nor distinguish the small songs
The birds bring him, calling with wide bills,
Out of the leaves and over the bare hills;
The squealing curlew and the loud thrush
Are both identical, just birds, birds;
He blames them sullenly as the agreed,
Ancestral enemies of the live seed,
Unwilling to be paid by the rich crop
Of music swelling thickly to the hedge top.

Blind? Yes, and deaf, and dumb, and the last irks most,
For could he speak, would not the glib tongue boast
A lore denied our neoteric sense,
Being handed down from the age of innocence?
Or would the cracked lips, parted at last, disclose
The embryonic thought that never grows?

SAINT ANTONY

Saint Antony in the sand saw shapes rising,
Formed by the wind, sinuous, lewd
As snakes dancing; their bitter poison
Entered the soul through his pale eyes.

Sleep came; the dances were renewed
Upon the retina, the lids not proof
Against the orgy of the spheres.
Night long he ranged the Bacchanalian dark,
Himself the prey, the hunter and the wood.

THE LABOURER

There he goes, tacking against the fields'
Uneasy tides. What have the centuries done
To change him? The same garments, frayed with light
Or seamed with rain, cling to the wind-scoured bones
And shame him in the eyes of the spruce birds.
Once it was ignorance, then need, but now
Habit that drapes him on a bush of cloud
For life to mock at, while the noisy surf
Of people dins far off at the world's rim.
He has been here since life began, a vague
Movement among the roots of the young grass.
Bend down and peer beneath the twigs of hair,
And look into the hard eyes, flecked with care;
What do you see? Notice the twitching hands,
Veined like a leaf, and tough bark of the limbs,
Wrinkled and gnarled, and tell me what you think.
A wild tree still, whose seasons are not yours,
The slow heart beating to the hidden pulse
Of the strong sap, the feet firm in the soil?
No, no, a man like you, but blind with tears
Of sweat to the bright star that draws you on.

THE LONELY FARMER

Poor hill farmer astray in the grass:
There came a movement and he looked up, but
All that he saw was the wind pass.
There was a sound of voices on the air,
But where, where? It was only the glib stream talking
Softly to itself. And once when he was walking
Along a lane in spring he was deceived
By a shrill whistle coming through the leaves:
Wait a minute, wait a minute—four swift notes;
He turned, and it was nothing, only a thrush
In the thorn bushes easing its throat.
He swore at himself for paying heed,
The poor hill farmer, so often again
Stopping, staring, listening, in vain,
His ear betrayed by the heart's need.

THE ONE FURROW

When I was young, I went to school
With pencil and foot-rule
Sponge and slate,
And sat on a tall stool
At learning's gate.

When I was older, the gate swung wide;
Clever and keen-eyed
In I pressed,
But found in the mind's pride
No peace, no rest.

Then who was it taught me back to go
To cattle and barrow,
Field and plough;
To keep to the one furrow,
As I do now?

FARM CHILD

Look at this village boy, his head is stuffed
With all the nests he knows, his pockets with flowers,
Snail-shells and bits of glass, the fruit of hours
Spent in the fields by thorn and thistle tuft.
Look at his eyes, see the harebell hiding there;
Mark how the sun has freckled his smooth face
Like a finch's egg under that bush of hair
That dares the wind, and in the mixen now
Notice his poise; from such unconscious grace
Earth breeds and beckons to the stubborn plough.

The Minister

Sŵn y galon fach yn torri

The Minister was broadcast on the Welsh Regional programme of the B.B.C. in 1952 and published in 1953 by the Montgomery Printing Company, Newtown.

Characters

NARRATOR	THE MINISTER
DAVIES	BUDDUG

In the hill country at the moor's edge
There is a chapel, religion's outpost
In the untamed land west of the valleys,
The marginal land where flesh meets spirit
Only on Sundays and the days between
Are mortgaged to the grasping soil.

This is the land of green hay
And greener corn, because of the long
Tarrying of winter and the late spring.
This is the land where they burn peat
If there is time for cutting it,
And the weather improves for drying it,
And the cart is not too old for carrying it
And doesn't get stuck in the wet bog.

This is the land where men labour
In silence, and the rusted harrow
Breaks its teeth on the grey stones.
Below, the valleys are an open book,
Bound in sunlight; but the green tale
Told in its pages is not true.

"Beloved, let us love one another," the words are blown
To pieces by the unchristened wind
In the chapel rafters, and love's text
Is riddled by the inhuman cry
Of buzzards circling above the moor.
Come with me, and we will go
Back through the darkness of the vanished years
To peer inside through the low window
Of the chapel vestry, the bare room
That is sour with books and wet clothes.

They chose their pastors as they chose their horses
For hard work. But the last one died
Sooner than they expected; nothing sinister,
You understand, but just the natural
Breaking of the heart beneath a load
Unfit for horses. "Ay, he's a good 'un,"
Job Davies had said; and Job was a master
Hand at choosing a nag or a pastor.

And Job was right, but he forgot,
They all forgot that even a pastor
Is a man first and a minister after,
Although he wears the sober armour
Of God, and wields the fiery tongue
Of God, and listens to the voice
Of God, the voice no others listen to;
The voice that is the well-kept secret
Of man, like Santa Claus,
Or where baby came from;
The secret waiting to be told
When we are older and can stand the truth.

O, but God is in the throat of a bird;
Ann heard Him speak, and Pantycelyn.
God is in the sound of the white water
Falling at Cynfal.   God is in the flowers
Sprung at the feet of Olwen, and Melangell
Felt His heart beating in the wild hare.
Wales in fact is His peculiar home,
 Our fathers knew Him. But where is that voice now?
Is it in the chapel vestry, where Davies is using
The logic of the Smithfield?

A young 'un we want, someone young
Without a wife. Let him learn
His calling first, and choose after
Among our girls, if he must marry.
There's your girl, Pugh; or yours, Parry;
Ministers' wives they ought to be
With those white hands that are too soft
For lugging muck or pulling a cow's
Tits. But ay, he must be young.
Remember that mare of yours, John?

Too old when you bought her; the old sinner
Had had a taste of the valleys first
And never took to the rough grass
In the top fields. You could do nothing
With her, but let her go her way.
Lucky you sold her. But you can't sell
Ministers, so we must have a care
In choosing. Take my advice,
Pick someone young, and I'll soon show him
How things is managed in the hills here.

NARRATOR

Did you notice the farm on the hill side
A bit larger than the others, a bit more hay
In the Dutch barn, four cows instead of two?
Prosperity is a sign of divine favour:
Whoever saw the righteous forsaken
Or his seed begging their bread? It even entitles
A chapel deacon to a tame pastor.

There were people here before these,
Measuring truth according to the moor's

Pitiless commentary and the wind's veto.
Out in the moor there is a bone whitening,
Worn smooth by the long dialectic
Of rain and sunlight. What has that to do
With choosing a minister? Nothing, nothing.

Thick darkness is about us, we cannot see
The future, nor the thin face
Of him whom necessity will bring
To this lean oasis at the moor's rim,
The marginal land where flesh meets spirit
Only on Sundays and the days between
Are mortgaged, mortgaged, mortgaged.
But we can see the faces of the men
Grouped together under the one lamp,
Waiting for the name to be born to them
Out of time's heaving thighs.

Did you dream, wanderer in the night,
Of the ruined house with the one light
Shining; and that you were the moth
Drawn relentlessly out of the dark?
The room was empty, but not for long.
You thought you knew them, but they always changed
To something stranger, if you looked closely
Into their faces. And you wished you hadn't come.
You wished you were back in the wide night
Under the stars. But when you got up to go
There was a hand preventing you.
And when you tried to cry out, the cry got stuck
In your dry throat, and you lay there in travail,
Big with your cry, until the dawn delivered you
And your cry was still-born and you arose and buried it,
Laying on it wreaths of the birds' songs.

But for some there is no dawn, only the light
Of the Cross burning up the long aisle
Of night; and for some there is not even that.

The cow goes round and round the field,
Bored with its grass world, and in its eyes
The mute animal hunger, which you pity,
You the confirmed sentimentalist,
Playing the old anthropomorphic game.
But for the cow, it is the same world over the hedge.
No one ever teased her with pictures of flyless meadows,
Where the grass is eternally green
No matter how often the tongue bruises it,
Or the dung soils it.

But with man it is otherwise.
His slow wound deepens with the years,
And knows no healing only the sharp
Distemper of remembered youth.

THE MINISTER

The Reverend Elias Morgan, B.A.:
I am the name on whom the choice fell.
I came in April, I came young
To the hill chapel, where long hymns were sung
Three times on a Sunday, but rarely between
By a lean-faced people in black clothes,
That smelled of camphor and dried sweat.

It was the time when curlews return
To lay their eggs in the brown heather.
Their piping was the spring's cadenza
After winter's unchanging tune.
But no one heard it, they were too busy

Turning the soil and turning the minister
Over and under with the tongue's blade.

My cheeks were pale and my shoulders bowed
With years of study, but my eyes glowed
With a deep, inner phthisic zeal,
For I was the lamp which the elders chose
To thaw the darkness that had congealed
About the hearts of the hill folk.

I wore a black coat, being fresh from college,
With striped trousers, and, indeed, my knowledge
Would have been complete, had it included
The bare moor, where nature brooded
Over her old, inscrutable secret.
But I didn't even know the names
Of the birds and the flowers by which one gets
A little closer to nature's heart.

Unlike the others my house had a gate
And railings enclosing a tall bush
Of stiff cypress, which the loud thrush
Took as its pulpit early and late.
Its singing troubled my young mind
With strange theories, pagan but sweet,
That made the Book's black letters dance
To a tune John Calvin never heard.
The evening sunlight on the wall
Of my room was a new temptation.
Luther would have thrown his Bible at it.
I closed my eyes, and went on with my sermon.

NARRATOR

A few flowers bloomed beneath the window,
Set there once by a kind hand

In the old days, a woman's gesture
Of love against the childless years.
Morgan pulled them up; they were untidy.
He sprinkled cinders there instead.

Who is this opening and closing the Book
With a bang, and pointing a finger
Before him in accusation?
Who is this leaning from the wide pulpit
In judgment, and filling the chapel
With sound as God fills the sky?
Is that his shadow on the wall behind?
Shout on, Morgan. You'll be nothing to-morrow.

The people were pleased with their new pastor;
Their noses dripped and the blood ran faster
Along their veins, as the hot sparks
Fell from his lips on their dry thoughts:
The whole chapel was soon ablaze.
Except for the elders, and even they were moved
By the holy tumult, but not extremely.
They knew better than that.

It was sex, sex, sex and money, money,
God's mistake and the devil's creation,
That took the mind of the congregation
On long journeys into the hills
Of a strange land, where sin was the honey
Bright as sunlight in death's hive.
They lost the parable and found the story,
And their glands told them they were still alive.
Job looked at Buddug, and she at him
Over the pews, and they knew they'd risk it
Some evening when the moon was low.

I know the place, under the hedge
In the top meadow; it was where my mam
Got into trouble, and only the stars
Were witness of the secret act.
They say her mother was the same.
Well, why not? It's hard on a girl
In these old hills, where youth is short
And boys are scarce; and the ones we'd marry
Are poor or shy. But Job's got money,
And his wife is old. Don't look at me
Like that, Job; I'm trying to listen
To what the minister says. Your eyes
Scare me, yet my bowels ache
With a strange frenzy. This is what
My mother and her mother felt
For the men who took them under the hedge.

NARRATOR

The moor pressed its face to the window.
The clock ticked on, the sermon continued.
Out in the fir-tree an owl cried
Derision on a God of love.
But no one noticed, and the voice burned on,
Consuming the preacher to a charred wick.

THE MINISTER

I was good that night, I had the *hwyl*.
We sang the verses of the last hymn
Twice. We might have had a revival
If only the organ had kept in time.
But that was the organist's fault.
I went to my house with the light heart
Of one who had made a neat job

Of pruning the branches on the tree
Of good and evil. Llywarch came with me
As far as the gate. Who was the girl
Who smiled at me as she slipped by?

NARRATOR

There was cheese for supper and cold bacon,
Or an egg if he liked; all of them given
By Job Davies as part of his pay.
Morgan sat down in his white shirt-sleeves
And cut the bacon in slices the way
His mother used to. He sauced each mouthful
With tasty memories of the day.
Supper over, can you picture him there
Slumped in his chair by the red fire
Listening to the clock's sound, shy as a mouse,
Pattering to and fro in the still house?
The fire voice jars; there is no tune to the song
Of the thin wind at the door, and his nearest neighbour
Being three fields' breadth away, it more often seems
That bed is the shortest path to the friendlier morrow.

But he was not unhappy; there were souls to save;
Souls to be rescued from the encroaching wave
Of sin and evil. Morgan stirred the fire
And drove the shadows back into their corners.

THE MINISTER

I held a *seiat*, but no one came.
It was the wrong time, they said, there were the lambs,
And hay to be cut and peat to carry.
Winter was the time for that.
Winter is the time for easing the heart,

85

For swapping sins and recalling the days
Of summer when the blood was hot.
Ah, the blurred eye and the cold vein
Of age! "Come home, come home. All is forgiven."

I began a Bible class;
But no one came,
Only Mali, who was not right in the head.
She had a passion for me, and dreamed of the day . . .
I opened the Bible and expounded the Word
To the flies and spiders, as Francis preached to the birds.

NARRATOR

Over the moor the round sky
Was ripening, and the sun had spread
Its wings and now was heading south
Over the sea, where Morgan followed.
It was August, the holiday month
For ministers; they walked the smooth
Pavements of Aber and compared their lot
To the white accompaniment of the sea's laughter.

THE MINISTER

When I returned, strengthened, to the bare manse
That smelled of mould, someone had broken a window
During my absence and let a bird in.
I found it dead, starved, on the warm sill.
There is always the thin pane of glass set up between us
And our desires.
We stare and stare and stare, until the night comes
And the glass is superfluous.
I went to my cold bed saddened, but the wind in the tree
Outside soothed me with echoes of the sea.

Harvest, harvest! The oats that were too weak
To hold their heads up had been cut down
And placed in stooks. There was no nonsense
Plaiting the last sheaf and wasting time
Throwing sickles. That was a fad of Prytherch
Of Nant Carfan; but the bugger was dead.
The men took the corn, the beautiful goddess,
By the long hair and threw her on the ground.

Below in the valleys they were thinking of Christmas;
The fields were all ploughed and the wheat in.
But Davies still hadn't made up his mind
Whom they should ask to the Thanksgiving.

The sea's tan had faded; the old pallor
Was back in Morgan's cheeks. In his long fight
With the bare moor, it was the moor that was winning.
The children came into Sunday School
Before he did, and put muck on his stool.
He stood for the whole lesson, pretending not to notice
The sounds in his desk: a mouse probably
Put there to frighten him. They loved their joke.
Say nothing, say nothing. Morgan was learning
To hold his tongue, the wisdom of the moor.
The pulpit is a kind of block-house
From which to fire the random shot
Of innuendo; but woe betide the man
Who leaves the pulpit for the individual
Assault. He spoke to Davies one day:

DAVIES

Adultery's a big word, Morgans: where's your proof?
You who never venture from under your roof

87

Once the night's come; the blinds all down
For fear of the moon's bum rubbing the window.
Take a word from me and keep your nose
In the Black Book, so it won't be tempted
To go sniffing where it's not wanted.
And leave us farmers to look to our own
Business, in case the milk goes sour
From your sharp talk before it's churned
To good butter, if you see what I mean.

NARRATOR

Did you say something?
Don't be too hard on them, there were people here
Before these and they were no better.
And there'll be people after may be, and they'll be
No better; it is the old earth's way
Of dealing with time's attrition.

Snow on the fields, snow on the heather;
The fox was abroad in the new moon
Barking. And if the snow thawed
And the roads cleared there was an election
Meeting in the vestry next the chapel.
Men came and spoke to them about Wales,
The land they lived in without knowing it,
The land that is reborn at such times.
  names;
They mentioned Henry Richard and S. R.—the great
And Keir Hardie; the names nobody knew.
It was quite exciting, but in the high marginal land
No names last longer than the wind
And the rain let them on the cold tombstone.
They stood outside afterwards and watched the cars
Of the speakers departing down the long road

To civilization, and walked home
Arguing confusedly under the stars.

THE MINISTER

Winter was like that; a meeting, a foxhunt,
And the weekly journey to market to unlearn
The lesson of Sunday. The rain never kept them
From the packed town, though it kept them from chapel.

> Drive on, farmer, to market
> With your pigs and your lean cows
> To the town, where the dealers are waiting
> And the girl in the green blouse,
> Fresh as a celandine from the spring meadows,
> Builds like a fabulous tale
> Tower upon tower on the counter
> The brown and the golden ale.

NARRATOR

A year passed, once more Orion
Unsheathed his sword from its dark scabbard;
And Sirius followed, loud as a bird
Whistling to eastward his bright notes.
The stars are fixed, but the earth journeys
By strange migrations towards the cold
Frosts of autumn from the spring meadows.
And we who see them, where have we been
Since last their splendour inflamed our mind
With huge questions not to be borne?

Morgan was part of the place now; he was beginning
To look back as well as forwards:
Back to the green valleys, forward along the track
That dwindled to nothing in the vast moor.

But life still had its surprises. There was the day
They found old Llywarch dead under the wall
Of the grey sheep-fold, and the sheep all in a ring
Staring, staring at the stiff frame
And the pursed lips from which no whistle came.

THE MINISTER

It was my biggest funeral of all; the hills crawled
With black figures, drawn from remote farms
By death's magnet. "So sudden. It might have been me."
And there in the cheap coffin Llywarch was lying,
Taller than you thought, and women were trying
To read through their tears the brass plate.

It might have been Davies! Quickly I brushed
The black thought away; but it came back.
My voice deepened; the people were impressed.
Out in the cold graveyard we sang a hymn,
O fryniau Caersalem; and the Welsh hills looked on
Implacably. It was the old human cry.
But let me be fair, let me be fair.
It was not all like this, even the moor
Has moods of softness when the white hair
Of the bog cotton is a silk bed
For dreams to lie on. There was a day
When young Enid of Gors Fach
Pressed an egg into my hand
Smiling, and her father said:
"Take it, Morgans, to please the child."
I never heard what they said after,
But went to my bed that night happy for once.
I looked from my top window and saw the moon,
Mellow with age, rising over the moor;
There was something in its bland expression
That softened the moor's harshness, stifled the questions

90

Struggling to my lips; I made a vow,
As other men in other years have done,
To-morrow would be different. I lay down
And slept quietly. But the morrow woke me
To the ancestral fury of the rain
Spitting and clawing at the pane.
I looked out on a grey world, grey with despair.

NARRATOR

The rhythm of the seasons: wind and rain,
Dryness and heat, and then the wind again,
Always the wind, and rain that is the sadness
We ascribe to nature, who can feel nothing.
The redwings leave, making way for the swallows;
The swallows depart, the redwings are back once more.
But man remains summer and winter through,
Rooting in vain within his dwindling acre.

THE MINISTER

I was the chapel pastor, the abrupt shadow
Staining the neutral fields, troubling the men
Who grew there with my glib, dutiful praise
Of a fool's world; a man ordained for ever
To pick his way along the grass-strewn wall
Dividing tact from truth.
                                        I knew it all,
Although I never pried, I knew it all.
I knew why Buddug was away from chapel.
I knew that Pritchard, the *Fron*, watered his milk.
I knew who put the ferret with the fowls
In Pugh's hen-house. I knew and pretended I didn't.
And they knew that I knew and pretended I didn't.
They listened to me preaching the unique gospel

Of love; but our eyes never met. And outside
The blood of God darkened the evening sky.

NARRATOR

Is there no passion in Wales? There is none
Except in the racked hearts of men like Morgan,
Condemned to wither and starve in the cramped cell
Of thought their fathers made them.
Protestantism—the adroit castrator
Of art; the bitter negation
Of song and dance and the heart's innocent joy—
You have botched our flesh and left us only the soul's
Terrible impotence in a warm world.

Need we go on? In spite of all
His courage Morgan could not avert
His failure, for he chose to fight
With that which yields to nothing human.
He never listened to the hills'
Music calling to the hushed
Music within; but let his mind
Fester with brooding on the sly
Infirmities of the hill people.
The pus conspired with the old
Infection lurking in his breast.

In the chapel acre there is a grave,
And grass contending with the stone
For mastery of the near horizon,
And on the stone words; but never mind them:
Their formal praise is a vain gesture
Against the moor's encroaching tide.
We will listen instead to the wind's text

Blown through the roof, or the thrush's song
In the thick bush that proved him wrong,
Wrong from the start, for nature's truth
Is primary and her changing seasons
Correct out of a vaster reason
The vague errors of the flesh.

Later Poems

Later Poems

CHILDREN'S SONG

We live in our own world,
A world that is too small
For you to stoop and enter
Even on hands and knees,
The adult subterfuge.
And though you probe and pry
With analytic eye,
And eavesdrop all our talk
With an amused look,
You cannot find the centre
Where we dance, where we play,
Where life is still asleep
Under the closed flower,
Under the smooth shell
Of eggs in the cupped nest
That mock the faded blue
Of your remoter heaven.

THE VILLAGE

Scarcely a street, too few houses
To merit the title; just a way between
The one tavern and the one shop
That leads nowhere and fails at the top
Of the short hill, eaten away
By long erosion of the green tide
Of grass creeping perpetually nearer
This last outpost of time past.

So little happens; the black dog
Cracking his fleas in the hot sun
Is history. Yet the girl who crosses
From door to door moves to a scale
Beyond the bland day's two dimensions.

Stay, then, village, for round you spins
On slow axis a world as vast
And meaningful as any poised
By great Plato's solitary mind.

LAMENT FOR PRYTHERCH

When I was young, when I was young!
Were you ever young, Prytherch, a rich farmer:
Cows in the byre, sheep in the pen,
A brown egg under each hen,
The barns oozing corn like honey?
You are old now; time's geometry
Upon your face by which we tell
Your sum of years has with sharp care
Conspired and crossed your brow with grief.
Your heart that is dry as a dead leaf
Undone by frost's cruel chemistry
Clings in vain to the bare bough
Where once in April a bird sang.

COLERIDGE

Walking often beside the waves'
Endless embroidery of the bare sand,
Coleridge never could understand,
Dazed by the knocking of the wind
In the ear's passage, the chorus
Of shrill voices from the sea
That mocked his vain philosophy
In salt accents. And at tide's retreat,
When the vexed ocean camping far
On the horizon filled the air
With dull thunder, ominous and low,
He felt his theories break and go
In small clouds about the sky,
Whose nihilistic blue repelled
The vain probing of his eye.

SONG AT THE YEAR'S TURNING

Shelley dreamed it. Now the dream decays.
The props crumble. The familiar ways
Are stale with tears trodden underfoot.
The heart's flower withers at the root.
Bury it, then, in history's sterile dust.
The slow years shall tame your tawny lust.

Love deceived him; what is there to say
The mind brought you by a better way
To this despair? Lost in the world's wood
You cannot stanch the bright menstrual blood.
The earth sickens; under naked boughs
The frost comes to barb your broken vows.

Is there blessing? Light's peculiar grace
In cold splendour robes this tortured place
For strange marriage. Voices in the wind
Weave a garland where a mortal sinned.
Winter rots you; who is there to blame?
The new grass shall purge you in its flame.

INVASION ON THE FARM

I am Prytherch. Forgive me. I don't know
What you are talking about; your thoughts flow
Too swiftly for me; I cannot dawdle
Along their banks and fish in their quick stream
With crude fingers. I am alone, exposed
In my own fields with no place to run
From your sharp eyes. I, who a moment back
Paddled in the bright grass, the old farm
Warm as a sack about me, feel the cold
Winds of the world blowing. The patched gate
You left open will never be shut again.

A PERSON FROM PORLOCK

There came a knocking at the front door,
The eternal, nameless caller at the door;
The sound pierced the still hall,
But not the stillness about his brain.
It came again. He arose, pacing the floor
Strewn with books, his mind big with the poem
Soon to be born, his nerves tense to endure
The long torture of delayed birth.

Delayed birth: the embryo maimed in the womb
By the casual caller, the chance cipher that jogs
The poet's elbow, spilling the cupped dream.

The encounter over, he came, seeking his room;
Seeking the contact with his lost self;
Groping his way endlessly back
On the poem's path, calling by name
The foetus stifling in the mind's gloom.

THE SLAVE

No offence, friend; it was the earth that did it.
Adam had Eve to blame; I blame the earth,
This brown bitch fawning about my feet.
My skin was a lily once like yours
Before she smirched it with her dirty ways
Blasting its petals with her cruel frost.
O, I would have had the deft tongue
To balance words with the precision
Of a clean stream, fingering stones.
But what could I do? She dragged me down,
Slurring my gait first, then my speech.
I never loved her, there's no ring
Binding us; but it's too late now.
I am branded upon the brow
With muck, as though I were her slave.
My clothes stink, where she has pressed
Her body to me, the lewd bawd,
Gravid as an old sow, but clawed.

TALIESIN 1952

I have been all men known to history,
Wondering at the world and at time passing;
I have seen evil, and the light blessing
Innocent love under a spring sky.

I have been Merlin wandering in the woods
Of a far country, where the winds waken
Unnatural voices, my mind broken
By sudden acquaintance with man's rage.

I have been Glyn Dŵr set in the vast night,
Scanning the stars for the propitious omen,
A leader of men, yet cursed by the crazed women
Mourning their dead under the same stars.

I have been Goronwy, forced from my own land
To taste the bitterness of the salt ocean;
I have known exile and a wild passion
Of longing changing to a cold ache.

King, beggar and fool, I have been all by turns,
Knowing the body's sweetness, the mind's treason;
Taliesin still, I show you a new world, risen,
Stubborn with beauty, out of the heart's need.

AUTUMN ON THE LAND

A man, a field, silence—what is there to say?
He lives, he moves, and the October day
Burns slowly down.
                              History is made
Elsewhere; the hours forfeit to time's blade
Don't matter here. The leaves large and small,
Shed by the branches, unlamented fall
About his shoulders. You may look in vain
Through the eyes' window; on his meagre hearth
The thin, shy soul has not begun its reign
Over the darkness. Beauty, love and mirth
And joy are strangers there.
                                        You must revise
Your bland philosophy of nature, earth
Has of itself no power to make men wise.

JANUARY

The fox drags its wounded belly
Over the snow, the crimson seeds
Of blood burst with a mild explosion,
Soft as excrement, bold as roses.

Over the snow that feels no pity,
Whose white hands can give no healing,
The fox drags its wounded belly.

THE POACHER

Turning aside, never meeting
In the still lanes, fly infested,
Our frank greeting with quick smile,
You are the wind that set the bramble
Aimlessly clawing the void air.
The fox knows you, the sly weasel
Feels always the steel comb
Of eyes parting like sharp rain
Among the grasses its smooth fur.
No smoke haunting the cold chimney
Over your hearth betrays your dwelling
In blue writing above the trees.
The robed night, your dark familiar,
Covers your movements; the slick sun,
A dawn accomplice, removes your tracks
One by one from the bright dew.

PRIEST AND PEASANT

You are ill, Davies, ill in mind;
An old canker, to your kind
Peculiar, has laid waste the brain's
Potential richness in delight
And beauty; and your body grows
Awry like an old thorn for lack
Of the soil's depth; and sickness there
Uncurls slowly its small tongues
Of fungus that shall, thickening, swell
And choke you, while your few leaves
Are green still.
              And so you work
In the wet fields and suffer pain
And loneliness as a tree takes
The night's darkness, the day's rain;
While I watch you, and pray for you,
And so increase my small store
Of credit in the bank of God,
Who sees you suffer and me pray
And touches you with the sun's ray,
That heals not, yet blinds my eyes
And seals my lips as Job's were sealed
Imperiously in the old days.

PISCES

Who said to the trout,
You shall die on Good Friday
To be food for a man
And his pretty lady?

It was I, said God,
Who formed the roses
In the delicate flesh
And the tooth that bruises.

THE RETURN

Coming home was to that:
The white house in the cool grass
Membraned with shadow, the bright stretch
Of stream that was its looking-glass;

And smoke growing above the roof
To a tall tree among whose boughs
The first stars renewed their theme
Of time and death and a man's vows.

A WELSHMAN TO ANY TOURIST

We've nothing vast to offer you, no deserts
Except the waste of thought
Forming from mind erosion;
No canyons where the pterodactyl's wing
Falls like a shadow.
The hills are fine, of course,
Bearded with water to suggest age
And pocked with caverns,
One being Arthur's dormitory;
He and his knights are the bright ore
That seams our history,
But shame has kept them late in bed.

THE LAST OF THE PEASANTRY

What does he know? moving through the fields
And the wood's echoing cloisters
With a beast's gait, hunger in his eyes
Only for what the flat earth supplies;
His wisdom dwindled to a small gift
For handling stock, planting a few seeds
To ripen slowly in the warm breath
Of an old God to whom he never prays.

Moving through the fields, or still at home,
Dwarfed by his shadow on the bright wall,
His face is lit always from without,
The sun by day, the red fire at night;
Within is dark and bare, the grey ash
Is cold now, blow on it as you will.

IN A COUNTRY CHURCH

To one kneeling down no word came,
Only the wind's song, saddening the lips
Of the grave saints, rigid in glass;
Or the dry whisper of unseen wings,
Bats not angels, in the high roof.

Was he balked by silence? He kneeled long,
And saw love in a dark crown
Of thorns blazing, and a winter tree
Golden with fruit of a man's body.

NO THROUGH ROAD

All in vain. I will cease now
My long absorption with the plough,
With the tame and the wild creatures
And man united with the earth.
I have failed after many seasons
To bring truth to birth,
And nature's simple equations
In the mind's precincts do not apply.

But where to turn? Earth endures
After the passing, necessary shame
Of winter, and the old lie
Of green places beckons me still
From the new world, ugly and evil,
That men pry for in truth's name.